America on the Brink!

A Nation Afflicted Before Final Judgment!

CHARLES PRETLOW

America on the Brink
A nation afflicted before final judgment!

November 2010

Copyright © Charles Pretlow

All rights reserved. Printed in the United States of America. No part of this publication may be reproduced, stored in a retrieval system, or transmitted, in any form or by any means electronic, mechanical, photocopying, recording, or otherwise, without the prior written permission of the author.

All scripture references and quotes are from the Revised Standard Version of the Holy Bible unless otherwise noted. Old Testament Section Copyright © 1952 New Testament Section Copyright © 1946, 1971 by Thomas Nelson Inc.

ISBN 978-0-9801768-3-4

Published by
Wilderness Voice Publishing
PO Box 857
Canon City, CO 81215

www.mcgmin.com

"A voice crying in the wilderness –
proclaiming the good news
of the coming Kingdom!"

Contents

When you see these things, straighten up	4
Judgment of the United States of America.	8
Birth pangs and false alarmists.	9
The devil wants the end to come early.	12
Buy from Christ gold refined by fire.	13
The cry of Job.	15
God allowed Job to lose everything	19
A nation afflicted before judgment.	23
The final harvest.	25
Prosperity, spiritualism, left-behind lie	27
The good news of the coming kingdom.	32
About the Author and Ministry Information	37
Charles Pretlow as Guest Speaker	38

Note: this message was first released in July of 2008, just before the 2008 economic crisis struck America.

When you see these things, straighten up!

How the second coming of Jesus Christ will unfold is a hot debate between many contemporary Christian authors and theologians. Unfortunately, most Christians have believed in a consensus of flawed theology concerning the rapture, the Great Tribulation, and the future of America.

There is a spell over the majority of sincere Christians, keeping their understanding darkened to the truth of Christ's return. Human nature wants to believe in the most favorable scenario concerning the end of this age and the coming of the Kingdom of God to earth.

The Apostle Paul warned, *"For the time is coming when people will not endure sound teaching, but having itching ears they will accumulate for themselves teachers to suit their own likings and will turn away from listening to the truth and wander into myths"* (2 Timothy 4:3,4).

Indeed, a great number of teachers preach myths and teach magic thinking doctrines concerning the things of God, especially how the end of this age will end. Few want to receive the truth laid out in Scripture, so false teachers pervert what Christ said concerning His coming. Most people like to hear soothing myths and conjecture about the most important event by God that is about to take place.

Of course, God knew this would be the case, so the end of this age will not come with a sudden bang! Christ said, "And when you hear of wars and tumults, do not be terrified; for this must first take place, but the end will not be at once" (Luke 21:9). What we are experiencing now, with all the earthquakes, wicked weather, wars, distress, and perplexity among the nations are what Christ called birth pangs.

These are merciful warnings allowed by God to break the spell over a multitude of deceived Christians and non-believers alike.

Many will not take these warnings to heart, rather pretend all the trouble will eventually die down and the nations will resolve their differences. Then there will be many Christians who awake to these signs but choose to believe the myth that Christ will rapture (remove the true Christian from the earth) before the coming trouble brings any real discomfort to them.

The nations of the world are perplexed with the extreme weather, earthquakes, ravaging floods, and hurricanes blamed by junk science as global warming. In truth, Jesus speaks of these events as birth pangs of the coming Kingdom of God. *"And there will be signs in sun and moon and stars, and upon the earth distress of nations in perplexity at the roaring of the sea and the waves, men fainting with fear and with foreboding of what is coming on the world; for the powers of the heavens will be shaken. And then they will see the Son of man coming in a cloud with power and great glory"* (Luke 21:25-27).

With years of wars and rumors of wars, the increase of perplexing issues in the Middle East, the renewal of the Cold War with Russia and China (few see this) and US economy on the brink of collapse, Christians should be awake and ready for the coming trouble leading to Christ's coming.

Yet a false peace and security keeps most Americans and Christians in a stupor. The gradual escalation of all these troubles has desensitized millions to the fact that the world is now on the brink of the Great Tribulation that leads to Armageddon.

The Apostle Paul wrote, *"But as to the times and the seasons, brethren, you have no need to have anything written to you. For you yourselves know well that the day of the Lord will come like a thief in the night. When people say, 'There is peace and security,' then sudden destruction will come upon them as travail comes upon a woman with child, and there will be no escape. But you are not in darkness, brethren, for that day to surprise you like a thief. For you are all sons of light and sons of the day; we are not of the night or of darkness. So then let us not sleep, as others do, but let us keep awake and be sober"* (1 Thessalonians 5:1-6).

Like lemmings headed for the cliff, masses of Christians along with the lost have bought into the false peace and security, and shudder with fear at God's warnings; the roaring of the seas, wars and rumors of wars, false teachers and false prophets, with the increase of gross wickedness matching that of Sodom and Gomorrah and as it was in the days of Noah.

God's people fear the truth, because they are not ready to give up the love of this world and submit to the Lordship of Christ. Many will be taken away in the coming sudden destruction. The delay in Christ's return and increased trouble is God trying to awaken His people from the spell of the false teachings before it is too late.

The birth pangs of the coming Kingdom are about to become terrifying. Even now, there is little that any nation can do at stopping the mounting worldwide political chaos and economic woes that are ever growing with intensity and frequency from wars, food shortages, earthquakes, floods, and killer storms.

All the nations are powerless in stopping the slide towards a worldwide economic collapse and global political chaos.

We are in the final days leading up to the Great Tribulation and most Christians are unprepared for what is about to take place.

Judgment of the United States of America
The end will come with the commencement of the Great Tribulation period. This final travail of trouble will be a major evangelistic tool in God's hands to gather in a multitude before the rapture, at the end of the Great Tribulation, just before the wrath of God falls upon the world. (See Revelation 7:9-14).

What will be the catalyst that ignites the end and mark the beginning of the Great Tribulation? The final judgment of the USA.

Few see judgment coming to America and those who have warned are maligned and ridiculed, even accused of being unpatriotic and divisive.

False peace and security, false doctrines, as well as extreme idolatry of the American dream have blinded most Christians to the reality that America has crossed the line of Biblical immorality and wickedness.

Russia and China are building their military prowess to attack America and control the world. The cold war is back and is hotter than ever. These two enemies of freedom and democracy believe that Communism will succeed only if they control the world and its resources. America is standing in the way of world dominance.

Once America is attacked and defeated, the end will begin. Few see this coming-few will be ready in time to endure such destruction and calamity.

Yes, when people will say, "There is peace and security" then sudden destruction will come!

Birth pangs and false alarmists

Many have warned over the last 40 years of a coming judgment to America. Few have taken these warnings to heart. Part of the reason for lack of sincere interest is due to false prophets, bandwagon soothsayers, and false alarmists soaking Christians with all manner of dates, prophecies, and wild speculations—being quite wrong.

Jesus warned about these false Christians leading many astray during the birth pangs of the coming Kingdom. *"Take heed that no one leads you astray. For many will come in my name, saying, 'I am the Christ,' and they will lead many astray. And you will hear of wars and rumors of wars; see that you are not alarmed; for this must take place, but the end is not yet. For nation will rise against nation, and kingdom against kingdom, and there will be famines and earthquakes in various places: all this is but the beginning of the birth-pangs"* (Matthew 24:4-8).

These so-called prophets heard nothing from the Lord, but only promoted fear and self-importance. Now, when true warnings are given, along with instructions for prayer and intercession, few take to heart the urgency of the hour, walk in fear of God, repent, and intercede for more time.

Rather, a panic consumes many, because the few who do take heed did little to become truly ready for the coming hardships. Now, when the trouble begins, many are tempted to save self and family, abandon millions of deceived Christians, and flee somewhere safe. Their trust in God wanes and clouds their senses and their judgment, like Israel trapped between the Pharaoh's army and the Red Sea. Loss of nerve and panic sets in as the sincere, but unprepared Christian looks for an avenue of escape.

God is saying to the true servant of Christ, standstill, and watch the salvation of God. This financial crisis and other afflictions is the beginning of judgment to shake millions awake who have believed lies concerning the end of the age sequences found in Scripture.

Satan knows this and wants to bring the end instantly, leaving masses of deceived Christians and sinners alike unprepared and thrown into the valley of decision and even premature death—consumed with unbelief, defiled, and lost in their trespasses.

Yes, millions of Christians are not ready to meet Christ and eternity, burdened with the cares of this life, in love with this world and following Christ in rote, religiously playing church, *"This people honors me with their lips, but their heart is far from me; in vain do they worship me, teaching as doctrines the precepts of men."*

And Christ warned, *"But take heed to yourselves lest your hearts be weighed down with dissipation and drunkenness and cares of this life, and that day come upon you suddenly like a snare; for it will come upon all who dwell upon the face of the whole earth. But watch at all times, praying that you may have strength to escape all these things that will take place, and to stand before the Son of man"* (Luke 21:34-36).

The devil wants the end to come early
Satan wants sincere, but deceived Christians to stay in a weighed down, deceived condition with the cares of this life blinding them to the hour, living for self—not for Christ. If the devil can suddenly push the end to come before its time, then he will have destroyed many of God's people.

Satan tried to kill Jesus before his time, had all the apostles arrested at the beginning of the church age, and tried to murder Peter before his time. However, God warned Joseph in a dream to flee taking Mary and baby Jesus to Egypt. Divine intervention came for the Apostles, as an angel of the Lord opened the prison doors and brought the apostles out with instructions to stand before the people in the temple and preach the Gospel! (See Acts 5:17-21, 12:1-17 concerning the apostles and Peter)

As for Herod's attempt to kill Peter to please the Jews, the church made earnest prayer for him. Thus, the very night that Herod was to bring Peter out to be executed, again the angel of the Lord appeared, slapped Peter on the side to awake him saying, "Get up quickly," leading Peter to safety, thus preempting another attempt by Satan to stop the Gospel from advancing.

This is the case now, the devil does not want the true Gospel of the Kingdom preached to the world before the end comes, as Jesus prophesied, *"And this gospel of the kingdom will be preached throughout the whole world, as a testimony to all nations; and then the end will come"* (Matthew 24:14).

These birth pang troubles, and the current economic crisis is God slapping His people awake saying, "Get ready quickly; there is much work to do." You and I have work to do, and if America falls completely instantly, it will not be accomplished. However, Satan wants the end to come early before God's people are awake and ready—to preempt the last move of God and final awakening with a sudden collapse and premature destruction of America.

We must pray earnestly for more time!

Buy from Christ gold refined by fire
Yes, God will allow Satan to crush America for its wickedness, including Christians who

played church, lived for self, and cared less about God's true purposes for America and the world.

Many equate America to the infamous Babylon of Revelation and rightly so, at least partially. The Babylon of John's end of the age revelation also includes other countries comprising an end-of-this-age greedy and politically corrupt commerce system. America, Britain, and the European Union lead this system, which has corrupted the nations of the world with this system's wealth and perverted-defiling cultures.

Because of America's wealth and prosperity, the church of America is steeped in self-righteous arrogance believing they are above others and are God's chosen. Yes, the Church of America has been used mightily throughout its history. Unfortunately, most Christians are in the condition described in the book of Revelation, convinced of being safe with Christ, but blind to the truth. Like the church of Laodicea, the Church of America (most Christians) think they are rich, prosperous and need nothing.

Jesus is saying to all of us, buy from Him gold refined by fire—meaning, embrace his chastening, be zealous for God's purposes and repent! A review of the message to the seven churches mentioned in Revelation Chapters two and three will give the sincere student of Scripture a picture of the condition that the Church of America has deteriorated to, regardless of denomination or fellowship preference.

The true Christian must understand and see that God will not rescue His people until the end of the Great Tribulation and we must be about doing God's perfect will while we are in exile on earth, awaiting Christ's appearance. We are to minister the Gospel through this end of age trouble and be used in a final great harvest of souls.

The birth pangs of the close of this age have been escalating, yet for so many Christians, life is at ease—until this crisis. God in his mercy is shaking everything to awaken a lukewarm, self-centered, self-righteous church before the start of the Great Tribulation.

The cry of Job

If we intercede, we may avoid complete collapse that will lead to anarchy, looting, martial law, and the end of capitalism and most of our freedoms.

If God hears our cries, instead of collapse, a recession will set in that will not be just another downturn business cycle, but a recession with rocky ups and downs leading to a depression, similar to the Great Depression where many investors lost their wealth overnight.

Perhaps there will be a momentary rebound, but this crisis is the beginning of judgment of America for its wickedness, greed, and immoral culture—and a Church in love with this world.

This current economic crisis is part of the increasing birth pangs to shake loose America's spell binding grip on God's people. This crisis is the start of a widespread economic hardship touching millions who thought they were well off, including many content and prosperous Christians. Bankruptcy, foreclosure, repossession, loss of employment, divorce, and hopelessness will be forced upon many. For many, standing in line for food stamps, handouts, and essentials will be the only way to survive. If we intercede, this judgment will be gradual, rather than overnight. (I believe God has granted this petition, but we must continue to cry out mercy and more time to get ready).

Politicians, economists, and financiers are at loss to correct the root problem caused by the greed that produced a staggering national debt, corrupt politicians, corrupt business executives, and lust for wealth through debt. America is sinking like the Titanic, and band-aids have helped slow the sinking, but now this crisis requires a tourniquet, not a band-aid, but even then, the inevitable end will only be postponed for a few more years, maybe ten to fifteen—if we do intercede now!

In the coming days, after this crisis dies down, a recession, now started, will worsen. A sputtering economy will suffer more stress due to the birth pangs Jesus predicted that mark the end of this age. *"And there will be signs in sun and moon and stars, and upon the earth distress of nations in perplexity at the roaring of the sea and the waves, men fainting with fear and with foreboding of what is coming on the world; for the powers of the heavens will be shaken. And then they will see the Son of man coming in a cloud with power and great glory. Now when these things begin to take place, look up and raise your heads, because your redemption is drawing near"* (Luke 21:25-28).

Yes, the powers of heaven are being shaken and Satan is about to come down in great wrath for he knows his time is short.

These stressful troubles will become very sobering, and the cry of Job will be heard from unprepared and lukewarm Christians throughout the land. God is allowing Satan to touch His people in this country and around the world. Many will blame God and not see the purpose or see that the god of this world is the perpetrator in the increasing misery.

Like the story of Job, Satan wanted to inflict trouble upon Job and destroy him—including taking his life. However, God allowed, in degrees, trouble to come upon Job at the hands of the devil. Job complained to God and to others that he did not deserve such treatment, that he had done right before God. The sudden swath of calamities baffled Job, and today the devil has been allowed to do the same. Job's complaint will be the case with many Christians and non-Christians alike.

Job cried out, *"Though I am innocent, I cannot answer him; I must appeal for mercy to my accuser. If I summoned him and he answered me, I would not believe that he was listening to my voice. For he crushes me with a tempest, and multiplies my wounds without cause; he will not let me get my breath, but fills me with bitterness. If it is a contest of strength, behold him! If it is a matter of justice, who can summon him?"* (Job 9:15-19).

Just as Job asked in frustration, soon millions will ask, "Why God, we thought we were exempt from suffering, and we would escape the coming trouble." Few understand the birth pang troubles that we are now experiencing, as well as the Great Tribulation is the wrath of Satan, not the wrath of God.

The world rejects God and many Christians walk in self-righteous arrogance in love with this world, some loving God as a second thought, or at best live for God believing they are exempt from trouble. America continues to reject God, as a self-righteous hypocritical church looks on, believing they are exempt from trouble. This rebellion and arrogance gives Satan a right to do his thing, as he did with Job.

God allowed Job to lose everything

In the book of James, God's purpose for allowing the devil to inflict such terrible trouble upon Job is revealed, *"Behold, we call those happy who were steadfast. You have heard of the steadfastness of Job, and you have seen the purpose of the Lord, how the Lord is compassionate and merciful"* (James 5:11).

God allowed the devil to inflict suffering upon Job, so He might bestow upon Job compassion and mercy! Initially, this may seem manipulative on God's part, but if we consider the alternative, indeed it is compassion and mercy. Job's problem, as with many today, is reliance on their belief in God as an insurance policy, making the premiums through self-righteous works leading to confidence in self, which often leads to religious arrogance. Blessings and prosperity become a signal to take it easy in life and often becoming a born-again Christian morph into a prideful stamp of approval by God to show off to others. Many even exhibit an "in your face" attitude, as we have certain national Christian leaders blaming homosexuals and witches as the cause for 9/11 or suggesting the US government assassinate Hugo Chávez.

Job's particular issues were along the lines of self-justification through self-reliance on his religious works. This gave Satan a right to sift and test Job. Job's condition of heart, if not corrected, could cause his faith to fail him.

Trusting in God while trusting in our own righteous living can nullify God's grace. The author of the book of Job makes clear the issue that allowed Satan to accost, sift, destroy, and almost physically kill Job, simply stated, "...because he was righteous in his own eyes" (Job 32:1). Elihu, the youngest of the four people trying to help Job see what all this suffering was about, finally convinced Job of this condition–Job was justifying himself rather than God.

Job was not sinning, but rather relying on his own righteousness to keep him in good standing with God; blessed, living prosperously, and protected. Satan sees this self-righteous stance, but God saw Job's true faith, in spite of Job's misunderstandings. In the end, when afflicted and then confronted, Job comes to a very needful realization about his relationship with God by stating, *"I had heard of thee by the hearing of the ear, but now my eye sees thee; therefore I despise myself, and repent in dust and ashes"* (Job 42:4,5).

Few Christian experience this true realization of self and come to salvation by grace through faith. Most do not see until they come to the end of themselves (as believers). The Apostle Paul conveys this important realization as well, when he wrote, *"Wretched man that I am! Who will deliver me from this body of death?"* (Romans 7:24).

Of course, Jesus Christ does for us and in us, what we, weakened by our human condition, cannot do. Few Christians truly experience coming to the end of their self-righteous inner stance, humbly changed in their inner most self, by God's grace, compassion, and mercy. Trouble, trials, and affliction serve God's purposes, to save the self-righteous from the same fatal mistake as that of the religious hypocritical Pharisees of Christ's day.

Many believers are in a smug, self-righteous condition far worse than Job, prideful and in love with this world, blind to the risk of being rejected by Christ. Many know of Christ, but few truly know him and He them. Jesus warned, "On that day many will say to me, 'Lord, Lord, did we not prophesy in your name, and cast out demons in your name, and do many mighty works in your name?' And then will I declare to them, 'I never knew you; depart from me, you evildoers.'" (Matthew 7:22-23).

Satan continues to prowl around like a roaring lion, seeking someone to destroy, and he will be more ferocious than ever; he is in the process of being cast out of heaven for good and he knows his time is short.

Like Job, the coming suffering is allowed by God to wake up millions of Christians, agnostics, atheists, and lost sinners alike and turn their hearts toward God—without doubt or reservation; becoming cleansed, changed, and looking to Christ and his soon appearance. In doing so, they will not be ensnared suddenly, but become prepared to endure to the end, *"But he who endures to the end will be saved"* (Matthew 24:13).

A nation afflicted before judgment

We must intercede during these times of crisis. As mentioned earlier, Satan is carrying out evil and it will get worse, *"Rejoice then, O heaven and you that dwell therein! But woe to you, O earth and sea, for the devil has come down to you in great wrath, because he knows that his time is short!"* (Revelation 12:12). This trouble and the coming Great Tribulation is not God's wrath, but the devil exercising destructive hate to work his diabolical plans, to take to hell as many as possible. Especially deceived Christians who think they will be raptured before the coming terrible time.

Satan is attempting to bring America down now, with complete collapse of the economy, financial systems, and civility in order to set up his lie to deceive millions who are ignorant of what is happening.

God's will is that no one should perish, but come to the saving knowledge of Christ and his soon return, that many would call on Him with all their heart, full of repentance and humble contrition. Many have faith, but that faith has been misdirected by a false gospel and lies that put them at ease with the belief that the end of the age is far off or the rapture comes before trouble.

Millions of believers are not ready, and if a sudden collapse occurs, with anarchy and destruction coming upon all, before they are warned and awaken to the truth, then many will follow the devil's plan, rather than endure trouble and keep their eternal salvation in Christ.

Our continuous prayer is that God does not abandon this nation and His people to sudden destruction—before the deceived multitudes are warned with the truth. Few realize what Christ said about his appearance in the clouds of heaven and the rapture of the true and ready Christian.

"Immediately after the tribulation of those days the sun will be darkened, and the moon will not give its light, and the stars will fall from heaven, and the powers of the heavens will be shaken; then will appear the sign of the Son of man in heaven, and then all the tribes of the earth will mourn, and they will see the Son of man coming on the clouds of heaven with power and great glory; and he will send out his angels with a loud trumpet call, and they will gather his elect from the four winds, from one end of heaven to the other" (Matthew 24:29-31).

The rapture occurs after the Great Tribulation, not prior. Then, after the rapture, the wrath of God comes upon those left upon the earth.

Leading up to the Great tribulation, will be more intense birth pangs; very troubling times to include wars, rumors of war, earthquakes, the roaring of the seas (hurricanes and wicked weather), and perplexities of the nations with confusion and hate leading to a crescendo of persecution towards Christians. We are praying for more time to get ready and warn during this ever-increasing time of affliction.

The valley of decision is awaiting millions, including ignorant and deceived believers. Satan wants to throw the multitudes into disarray and hopelessness by keeping the truth hidden by false doctrine and false leaders throughout Christianity. The devil desires to start his work and plans before God's people are ready, awake, and no longer deceived.

The final harvest

"Multitudes, multitudes, in the valley of decision! For the day of the LORD is near in the valley of decision" (Joel 3:14) and, *"After this I looked, and behold, a great multitude which no man could number, from every nation, from all tribes and peoples and tongues, standing before the throne and*

before the Lamb, clothed in white robes, with palm branches in their hands, and crying out with a loud voice, 'Salvation belongs to our God who sits upon the throne, and to the Lamb!' ... Then one of the elders addressed me, saying, 'Who are these, clothed in white robes, and whence have they come?' I said to him, 'Sir, you know.' And he said to me, 'These are they who have come out of the great tribulation; they have washed their robes and made them white in the blood of the Lamb. Therefore are they before the throne of God, and serve him day and night within his temple; and he who sits upon the throne will shelter them with his presence. They shall hunger no more, neither thirst any more; the sun shall not strike them, nor any scorching heat. For the Lamb in the midst of the throne will be their shepherd, and he will guide them to springs of living water; and God will wipe away every tear from their eyes.'" (Revelation 7:9-17).

This is our last call to get ready. This crisis must not be allowed to turn into the devil's plan to prematurely start the end. It is God's will for this crisis to subside, nevertheless this is the beginning of the end, for when America falls—a world-wide chaos follows, making way for the anti-Christ rule and the start of the

Great Tribulation. With all this trouble a multitude will come to the true Christ.

Prosperity, spiritualism, and the left-behind lie!

Why are millions of sincere Christians asleep and unprepared? Most believe Christianity and the work of the church will usher in the coming of the Kingdom of God, or the rapture will occur before the Great Tribulation.

There are three major false teachings holding true believers at risk of having their faith weakened and even made shipwreck.

1.) The word of faith, prosperity message promoted by pretentious (self-exalted) teachers, who have made the way of truth reviled. Peter prophesied of this insidious work of the devil by prophesying, *"But false prophets also arose among the people, just as there will be false teachers among you, who will secretly bring in destructive heresies, even denying the Master who bought them, bringing upon themselves swift destruction. And many will follow their licentiousness, and because of them the way of truth will be reviled. And in their greed they will exploit you with false words; from of old their condemnation has not been idle, and their destruction has not been asleep"* (2 Peter 2:1-3).

These false teachers preach that godliness is a way to get rich, exercising false faith to bring prosperity and wealth, but in reality, it is disguised as greed and the love of money. Paul wrote, *"If any one teaches otherwise and does not agree with the sound words of our Lord Jesus Christ and the teaching which accords with godliness, he is puffed up with conceit, he knows nothing; ... imagining that godliness is a means of gain. There is great gain in godliness with contentment; for we brought nothing into the world, and we cannot take anything out of the world; but if we have food and clothing, with these we shall be content. But those who desire to be rich fall into temptation, into a snare, into many senseless and hurtful desires that plunge men into ruin and destruction. For the love of money is the root of all evils; it is through this craving that some have wandered away from the faith and pierced their hearts with many pangs"* (1 Timothy 6:3-10).

2.) Counterfeit faith movements produce maddening spiritualistic experiences that deceive many naïve and ignorant believers. Many embrace teachings that promote beliefs that Christians will influence the world in a great movement of the Holy Spirit, so powerful that it will usher in the next millennial age with little trouble. The Apostle

Paul warned of this stating, *"But understand this, that in the last days there will come times of stress. For men will be lovers of self, lovers of money, proud, arrogant, abusive, disobedient to their parents, ungrateful, unholy, inhuman, implacable, slanderers, profligates, fierce, haters of good, treacherous, reckless, swollen with conceit, lovers of pleasure rather than lovers of God, holding the form of religion but denying the power of it. Avoid such people. For among them are those who make their way into households and capture weak women, burdened with sins and swayed by various impulses, who will listen to anybody and can never arrive at a knowledge of the truth. As Jannes and Jambres opposed Moses, so these men also oppose the truth, men of corrupt mind and counterfeit faith; but they will not get very far, for their folly will be plain to all, as was that of those two men... Indeed all who desire to live a godly life in Christ Jesus will be persecuted, while evil men and impostors will go on from bad to worse, deceivers and deceived"* (2 Timothy 3:1-13).

These so-called movements of the Holy Spirit are counterfeit, a satanic attempt to undermine and dilute the coming true move of God that will lead to the final harvest during the Great Tribulation. They teach against sanctification, trials, and the discipline of the Lord, thus denying the power of the Gospel of Christ to produce true character change. Many of the leaders have been exposed as pleasure seekers, some caught in perverse sin and fraud. Many are imposters who have counterfeit faith that produce signs and wonders that are not of God. Like the magicians in the Pharaohs court who opposed Moses, they used demonic power and kept up with the spiritual power of God for the first three plagues. Many are deceived, becoming more crazed with the lust for power, as they deceive the many.

3.) Rapture before trouble – the left-behind lie. This false doctrine has put millions of Christians to sleep and at ease. This teaching promoted by the left behind series of books and movies by authors Tim LaHaye and Jerry Jenkins, and other books such as The Late Great Planet Earth by Hal Lindsey have seduced millions of Christians to believe an outright lie that totally contradicts Christ's words. Quoting Christ from the Gospel of Mark, Scripture clearly explains when the rapture occurs, *"But in those days, after that tribulation... then they will see the Son of man coming in clouds with great power and glory. And then he will send out the angels, and gather his elect from the four winds, from the ends of the earth to the ends of heaven"* (Mark 13:24-27).

The Apostle Paul confirms the truth of the rapture by writing, *"But as to the times and the seasons, brethren, you have no need to have anything written to you. For you yourselves know well that the day of the Lord will come like a thief in the night. When people say, 'There is peace and security,' then sudden destruction will come upon them as travail comes upon a woman with child, and there will be no escape. But you are not in darkness, brethren, for that day to surprise you like a thief. For you are all sons of light and sons of the day; we are not of the night or of darkness. So then let us not sleep, as others do, but let us keep awake and be sober. For those who sleep sleep at night, and those who get drunk are drunk at night. But, since we belong to the day, let us be sober, and put on the breastplate of faith and love, and for a helmet the hope of salvation. For God has not destined us for wrath, but to obtain salvation through our Lord Jesus Christ, who died for us so that whether we wake or sleep we might live with him"* (1 Thessalonians 5:1-10).

Here Paul says that we are to stay awake and sober minded so that Christ's appearance does not take us by surprise. This passage does not say we will escape the Great Tribulation but escape the wrath of God.

Elsewhere Paul writes, *"For this we declare to you by the word of the Lord, that we who are alive, who are left until the coming of the Lord, shall not precede those who have fallen asleep. For the Lord himself will descend from heaven with a cry of command, with the archangel's call, and with the sound of the trumpet of God. And the dead in Christ will rise first; then we who are alive, who are left, shall be caught up together with them in the clouds to meet the Lord in the air; and so we shall always be with the Lord. Therefore comfort one another with these words"* (1 Thessalonians 4:15-18).

Yes, there will be the rapture, sometime after the Great Tribulation and the anti-Christ rule starts, and just before the wrath of God comes upon the earth.

Christ said that tribulation period would be cut short: *"And if those days had not been cut short, no human being would be saved. But for the sake of the elect those days will be cut short"* Matthew 24:22

The good news of the coming kingdom
Before all this begins, the good news of the coming Kingdom will be preached to the

whole world. This means that the true end-time scenario, as described in Scripture, will be brought to the forefront as the birth pangs lead to the start of the Great Tribulation.

During the coming trouble, Jesus warned of many false prophets coming with great signs and wonders to deceive the masses, tricking many to follow the antichrist bailout government, promising peace, and prosperity.

The coming time we have left must be used to get ready and be used in the last great outpouring of the Holy Spirit, promoting the truth of Christ's return. Many will be persecuted and even martyred by those who oppose the truth, just as Jesus warned, *"Then they will deliver you up to tribulation, and put you to death; and you will be hated by all nations for my name's sake. And then many will fall away, and betray one another, and hate one another. And many false prophets will arise and lead many astray. And because wickedness is multiplied, most men's love will grow cold. But he who endures to the end will be saved. And this gospel of the kingdom will be preached throughout the whole world, as a testimony to all nations; and then the end will come"* (Matthew 24:9-14).

We have much work to do—pray for more time to get ready! The true saint will not be raptured until his or her work is done. In the above passage Jesus warned of a great falling away, where Christian will betray Christian. Already the far left in this country detest evangelical Christians who truly follow Christ.

As trouble and shaking increase more Christians will begin to look up and realize the truth. The true Christian in the coming hour will begin to evangelize other Christians and the lost by pronouncing the coming of the Great Tribulation and Christ's soon appearance in the clouds.

The truth will be preached with such fervor and power, inspired, and led by the Holy Spirit that millions will be startled and stunned. A true move of God will begin that won't be around a teacher, or leader of a denomination, but on the truth of Christ's soon return.

True signs and wonders will accompany these Christians and new leaders will emerge who preach sound doctrine, help disciple, and mentor others, and avoid leadership idolatry. They will preach the cross and its work within the believer's life.

The world and media coverage will be amazed and even dumbfounded at first. The eyes of the world will momentarily be fixed on this true and final move of God. Many false Christian leaders will denounce this as fanaticism and oppose the message. Some who do this will end up like Ananias and Sapphira or Elymas the Magician.

Then as predicted, the message will have been heard around the world by all nations. Persecution madness will overtake the unbelieving world and these true Christians will be hated, maligned, ridiculed, and even martyred. Then the judgment of America will come suddenly—then you will see the antichrist step into power and be proclaimed as the world peacemaker, then the Great Tribulation will start.

There is a small window of time to work, we must not squander that time: "*Look carefully then how you walk, not as unwise men but as wise, making the most of the time, because the days are evil"* (Ephesians 5:15, 16).

Let us become truly ready, grow up into the true Christ and be used of God on the day that acts. We encourage you to pass this message on.

Recommended action: If the Holy Spirit bears witness to this message and you believe that acting now is prudent, then consider the following:

☦ Pray earnestly, consistently, and partner with likeminded believers in intercessory prayer.

☦ If you cannot find a likeminded fellowship, then consider starting a home gathering with likeminded believers.

☦ Share with others who are open to the truth, do not force this on those who are closed, rather pray, and wait for God to open their eyes. Learn to work with those whom God is working with.

☦ Seek the Lord for help in dealing with any carnal attitudes, fears, insecurities, and of course sin that may trouble you. Buy from Christ gold refined in fire—this means embrace his discipline that helps cleanse us from defilements and learn how to crucify the works of the flesh.

☦ Prepare for the future by learning to rely on God, not self, others, the government, or investing in uncertain (risky) riches. Get out of debt; seek wisdom from above and direction concerning safety for you and your family. Be willing to relocate if God so directs. Regardless, if you earnestly cry out to God, He will make a way and deliver you from the coming trouble or guide you through the fires.

† If open, share this message with your leadership, but do not push it on those who scoff at the truth—you will only be abused. *"He who corrects a scoffer gets himself abuse, and he who reproves a wicked man incurs injury. Do not reprove a scoffer, or he will hate you; reprove a wise man, and he will love you"* (Proverbs 9:7,8).

About Charles Pretlow and MC Global Ministries

It was in 1973, when Charles accepted Christ, just after his reenlistment in the Marines for six more years. Then in 1974, after reading David Wilkerson's book The Vision, he accepted Christ's call to full time ministry and requested an early release from the Corps. Miraculously, his honorable discharge was granted.

In January of 1975 he began Bible College and accepted his first ministry appointment. His years of formal education and leadership training have helped him in ministry. However, his more in-depth training, wisdom, and character development were honed through years of ministering in a wilderness type training, facilitated by Jesus in the discipline of the Lord.

His call is to help Christians become tribulation proof and rapture ready. Most Christians are not prepared for the coming troubles that God will use to make His church "without spot or blemish"—if you will, to become rapture ready.

Contacting MC Global Ministries

If you are seriously looking for messages that are sound in doctrine to help you get ready and desire genuine fellowship, then perhaps MC Global Ministries may be able to help you.

We mean business and our faces are set as flint concerning the call set before us. If you desire to change the direction God has given us or argue over the message of repentance, sanctification, and how to endure the coming Great Tribulation, then contacting us would not be beneficial.

However, if you are teachable and hungry to learn how to allow the true Christ to change you through his loving discipline, then this ministry can help you.

Contact Information

Mailing address:
MC Global Ministries
PO Box 857, Canon City, CO 81215
www.mcgmin.com   contact@mcgmin.com

Pastor Pretlow as Guest Speaker

Charles has garnered over thirty-five years of preaching the Word, teaching sound doctrine, counseling, and leadership mentoring. A Pastor, a self-published author, and one of the founders of MC Global Ministries.

The following are topics to consider for your fellowship or conference event:

- The Midnight Cry Awakening.
- Growing Up into Salvation.
- The Holy Spirit, the Gift, Gifts, Baptism, and Fruit.
- Exposing Darkness.
- Recovery for God's Wounded.
- God's Recovery Program.
- Christ's School of Ministry.
- Protecting the Ninety-Nine.
- Special Topics can be requested.

www.ingramcontent.com/pod-product-compliance
Lightning Source LLC
Chambersburg PA
CBHW070751050426
42449CB00010B/2429